D1046001

# Lasso the Sunshine

# Lasso the Sunshine
## Capture the Brighter Side of Life
by
## Bob Farmer, MD

Farmer, Robert T.
Lasso the Sunshine/ Capture the Brighter Side of Life

ISBN# 0-9787859-0-8

Every effort has been made to acknowledge authors of previous works, as well as to give intellectual credit as appropriate to statements or remarks attributed to other individuals.

*Lasso the Sunshine* and *Lasso the Sunshine- Capture the Brighter Side of Life* are trademark and copyright protected.

The poems *A Child's Smile, Reflections of Heaven, My Angel* and *My Family* are also copyright protected.

No portion of this text may be reproduced or distributed without permission from the author.

Copyright © 2004 by Bob Farmer
All Rights Reserved.

Here's to hoping everyone, in whatever endeavors, can lasso the sunshine and capture the brighter side of life. I certainly have…

Bob Farmer

# Acknowledgements

Three indisputable facts exist in the world: the sun rises in the east, it sets in the west, and it has shone down favorably upon me. I was born into a loving family in the United States of America with all of my parts in place and a good head on my shoulders. I have never been in want or need of anything. I have been blessed with good health, and I am truly happy. I married my high school sweetheart, Christina, and we have three wonderful children – Austin, Alexis, and Ashleigh. They bring joy into my life every single day, and can even change cloudy days into sunny ones.

God blessed me with a wonderful childhood. My parents, Ted and Virginia, worked hard to provide countless opportunities for me and my brother, Alan. They are wonderful role models and genuinely great people. If every kid were lucky enough to have my parents, the world would be a better place. I hope I can do for my children all that my mom and dad did and continue to do for me. I do not tell them often enough, but I have tremendous love and respect for them.

My brother, Alan, is kind of to me what Wally Cleaver was to the Beaver. He is a big brother who showed his little brother the right path, having also paved it along the way to make my journey a little easier. I look up to him and respect him, and feel a great sense of pride when asked if he is my brother. He is the best big brother a guy could ask for, and I love him dearly.

My children are my inspiration, my heart, and my soul. They are truly a gift from heaven, delivered by angels to remind me why I am here. The stresses of the world are somehow put on hold by a child's hug or smile. In the pages that follow, it will become quite evident that they are the light that brightens my world.

I have known my wife, Christina, since the fourth grade. She is the most honest, giving, and selfless person I know. She places the interests of others ahead of her own. She is a beautiful person on the outside, but her inner beauty exceeds even that. I suspect God took the best traits from his most prized angels when he drew up her blueprints. She inspires and encourages me. She is the world's best mom to our children. She is my best friend, and I thank God for her every day.

I would be remiss if I did not thank those who helped teach me how to read and write, and, in general, just a lot about life. I am referring to my teachers and coaches. I have been blessed with many dedicated and fantastic instructors. Some of my writing instructors may cringe at the occasional fragmented or run-on sentences, dangling prepositions, incongruent possessives, etc. I assure them all were done for effect. Call it artistic license, if you will.

I must also mention and thank another group – our military veterans and active duty. I am able to write freely in the comforts and privacy of my home because of their sacrifices. My grandfather served in the European theater of World War II as a forward observer. He never would speak much about it, other than to say that a lot of good men died. Every young student should be required to walk through Arlington National Cemetery as part of a civics or U.S. History curriculum. Its landscape is one of the most moving and powerful on earth. Seemingly endless rolling hills of cotton-white headstones leave an enduring image etched in one's brain. Nearby, on the National Mall in Washington, D.C., stands the Korean War Memorial. At the apex of an expanding triangle of life-size soldiers, boldly etched in granite, are the words, "Freedom is not Free." Even today, as we are in a long-term war against terrorism, I am thankful for those men and women who choose to protect us, and the words of the Korean War Memorial ring timeless.

My life is truly a wonderful one. My family and friends make it easy for me to lasso the sunshine. It is my hope that with this book I can convey that message to others, and help them, too, capture the brighter side of life!

# Table of Contents

# Sunrise

Do you remember the mythology you learned as a child? I suspect you were probably sitting in a junior high or high school literature or ancient civilizations class wishing you were somewhere else. Perhaps you recall (or maybe you do not) the story of the Greek god Helios and his impetuous son, Phaeton. Helios was the God of the Sun. He was responsible for the sun's daily journey across the sky. Every day Helios would fly his golden chariot and team of horses from east to west, pulling the sun along and illuminating the earth. One day, Phaeton, much to his father's dismay, boarded the chariot of the sun and headed across the sky. He held in his grasp the reins of that star that is paramount and indeed essential to our existence on the planet – the sun. He found it to be much too powerful to control, lost a handle over the stallions, and the sun raced erratically across the sky. It plunged dangerously close to the earth, scorching it in some areas leaving deserts behind. Zeus, the King of the Gods himself, had to intervene to save the planet. Phaeton failed to recognize the power he held in his hands.

The sun is all-powerful. It is the provider of light, the provider of warmth, the provider of energy. Without the sun, there is no life. Without the sun, crops will not grow, flowers will not bloom, and a trip to the beach seems to lose its appeal. Without the sun, we would all be kept in the dark, literally.

Much like Helios, we too can take the reins of the sun in our hands. Better yet, we can lasso the sun and pull it directly into our grasp. We must be wary, however, not to become brash and careless, or we could meet Phaeton's fate. We must understand the power the sun holds, learn from what it can teach us, respect it, and then apply its principles. Simply by approaching life with a daily goal of lassoing the sunshine, we can find the brighter side of all we encounter in life. We should strive to attain those characteristics of the sun that make it so vital, and then apply those characteristics to our approach to daily living.

How wonderful it would be to shed some light on perhaps once complicated issues; to feel energized and revitalized when we awaken each day – just like the rising sun! Lassoing the sun's characteristics will allow one to feel a sense of warmth and satisfaction when perhaps a different attitude would yield a sense of distress or self-pity.

The following chapters attempt to provide a framework by which you can introduce those characteristics of the sun into your life. Doing so will ultimately lead to a happier, less stressful, and more productive life. Instead of focusing on those aspects of daily life that are bad, worse, and the worst, you can focus on the brighter side – the good, the better, and the best life has to offer. You will be able to take almost any situation and derive something positive from it. First, however, you must make the decision and commitment – the decision and commitment to lasso the sunshine and capture the brighter side of life!

# Quit Complaining
## and
# Count Your Blessings

My inspiration to write this book was derived from observations I began to make during my days in college, medical school, and subsequently a medical residency program in family medicine. I encountered many people, including myself, who seemed to find it easy to become entrenched in self-pity when confronted with a challenging hurdle on life's track.

I recall still being awake at three a.m. cramming for a biochemistry final exam as a junior in college at the University of Illinois. At the time I was frustrated with the material (most of which has long been forgotten) and feeling sorry for myself for having to stay up so late to learn it. How pitiful I was! Poor me! Sitting there in a warm, safe dormitory room next to empty pizza boxes and several two liter bottles of caffeinated cola obtaining a Big Ten education financed by my parents' hard work. Poor me! Me and countless others facing such trying conditions. We were a bunch of spoiled boys and girls at the big university who found plenty of time for countless diversions to studying, yet wondered why we felt nervous the night before the exam. Looking back it really is quite embarrassing. How could I have been so blessed (and still am) in life and resort to self-pity due to a biochemistry test?

Unfortunately, the pity did not stop there. It is an undeniable fact that the further one travels on the road to obtaining a medical degree and eventually completing a residency program, the more one utilizes the self-pity defense mechanism. It is rather paradoxical to consider that the closer one gets to completing the training to become a physician – a profession with tremendous reward and fulfillment on many fronts – the more many feel sorry for themselves.

I found myself on call and required to stay overnight at the hospital on both Christmas Day and New Year's Eve during my first year of residency training. For someone who had spent every Christmas in my life prior to this one with family, this had the makings of a self-pity extravaganza. Instead, it was a turning point. It was on that Christmas Day when I first learned to lasso the sunshine!

Sure, I was on call and required to stay at the hospital on Christmas Day. So what? How many millions would have traded me places in an instant? I needed to endure a relatively mild amount of personal sacrifice in return for all of the benefits that accompany the role of physician in our society – easy choice. What triggered such a change in attitude? The CBS Evening News. A great many hours while on call were spent sitting in a room we residents appropriately referred to as the "call room." It had all of the essentials for a night on call in the hospital – a couch, a bathroom, a television, and a phone. Some nights it seemed I never put down the phone, spending countless hours dealing with patient care issues. Other nights were spent vegetating in front of the television. My Christmas Day call was rather slow. It seems many patients put off or ignore their heart attacks or kidney stones until after the holiday. I was eating that world famous cuisine all hospitals are known for while watching the evening news. Just as I was complaining to myself about my meal, a story detailing the civil war in Bosnia came across the screen. The news was bleak; killing, ethnic cleansing, starvation, children left orphaned, destruction of entire cities, peacekeepers coming under attack. I found a new perspective.

Sitting in that call room on that Christmas Day, I found myself engaging in some serious introspection. Recognizing my propensity that day and in the past to resort to self-pity, I decided then and there enough was enough.

The time had come to lasso the sunshine. The time had come to embrace the opportunity the Lord had given me. I had been given the chance to help others who were ailing. I had been given the chance to be a doctor! Yes, maybe I had to work on Christmas, and maybe I had to stay at the hospital for a thirty-six hour shift. But reflecting upon the overwhelming positives of my chosen field, how could I possibly focus on an occasional negative? To do so would have been counterproductive.

Rounding on patients with my previous self-pitying attitude could have proven to be a long and horrendous day. Instead I took advantage of the time to try to help and add some humor and smiles to those who were ill. How dare I feel sorry for myself when I was healthy and others were sick. I spent more time with each patient that day. Some of the time was focused on their illness, but most of it was spent just visiting. I enjoyed that. God was telling me something that Christmas, and I was listening. I learned on Christmas Day, 1995 to lasso the sunshine and capture the brighter side of a given situation. I have always been happy, but I have been even happier since then.

# The Theory of Relativity

Albert Einstein is not considered one of the most brilliant minds the world has ever seen for nothing. His theory of relativity helped to revolutionize the way we viewed the world around us. We, too, can use the theory of relativity to change our lives. Okay, it is not the same theory of relativity, but the same concept applies.

Einstein used his theory to demonstrate the relationship two objects have with respect to one another in the physical world. We will use our theory to examine the relative conditions in which one may find oneself. We will use this theory to remind ourselves that no situation is as bleak as it may at first appear. As mentioned earlier, I first learned to apply this principle on Christmas Day, 1995, when I was on a thirty-six hour call at the hospital. At the very point when I was feeling most sorry for myself, I saw a newscast on the nightly report documenting the abhorrent conditions the people of Bosnia were enduring as a result of civil war. Families were without food or shelter during the peak of winter. Many children were without families, left orphaned by the scourge of war. American soldiers were there as well, sent to keep the "peace." They, too, were without their families, risking their lives to help save others. They risked orphaning their children back home while trying to prevent other children from suffering the same fate.

I was embarrassed and ashamed that I had ever complained about anything in my life. I had never been in want of anything. I had never known what it was like to feel the pangs of hunger, the chill of unrelenting cold, or the wonder of where I might sleep that night. Quite the contrary. I grew up in the comforts of middle class America. I worried about what my mom had made for dinner that evening. Was my Izod shirt still in style? Should I sleep with the electric blanket or down comforter tonight? The scraps we gave our beagle and rat terrier would have been a precious commodity in other parts of the world.

Reflecting on many of the thoughts in the call room at the hospital, it was blatantly clear to me that self-pity served no purpose other than to bring myself and those around me down. Emotions can be contagious. Actions can be contagious. If a high school basketball team is being dominated going into halftime, an inspiring locker-room speech by the coach may be the spark needed to inspire a second half rally. On the other hand, a speech scolding the players could further a defeatist attitude and insure failure. If I had chosen to walk around the hospital all day complaining about how unfair it was that I was on call, no doubt others would start complaining too. I truly believe that because I projected a positive attitude that Christmas Day, others around me felt better as well.

One person's trials and tribulations may be viewed as a luxury by others. I was the young medical intern upset about being on call. My situation would have been gladly sought after by the medical student struggling just to make it through medical school. And his dilemma would have been welcomed by the fourth year college student attempting to get interviews to get into medical school. Or how about the person who wants to go to college but cannot afford it?

Such situations all serve to demonstrate why understanding the theory of relativity is so important. Remembering that there are those who would gladly be in your position should serve to put the challenges one encounters on a daily basis into better perspective.

Even in the seemingly worst of circumstances there exist great examples of human survival by people looking beyond their current predicament. Through the powers of hope, faith, love, imagination, and creativity they not only endure the greatest of human challenges, but also take from the situation a better understanding of themselves, and almost always a better appreciation for life and its blessings.

Most people are familiar with the truly inspirational story of actor Christopher Reeve and his wife, Dana. In life and in death they both demonstrated the frailty of the human body and the limitless power of the human spirit.

As an actor, Christopher Reeve was well known for his role as the superhero, Superman. In real life he suffered a cervical spinal cord injury during an equestrian event that left him paralyzed from the neck down and dependent on a ventilator to help him breathe. During an interview with Paula Zahn on CNN, Reeve recounted the challenges he faced in the years after his accident. While initially struggling with paralysis and all of its life altering implications, over time he was able to come to terms with the situation. He went through grief, self-pity, despair, and at one point even suicidal ideations. Eventually he asked himself, "What do we do afterwards. How do we find the meaning?" He answered his own question, stating that if one views such a tragic event "… as an opportunity, not as a complete disaster, then you can get things done."

Reeve was fortunate that he did not have to face his future alone. For a person who had been so self-sufficient all of his life to now have to rely on someone else for just about everything was going to be very difficult. He learned a lot about himself. He learned a lot about patience. He learned a lot about communication. He credited his wife, Dana, for helping him to get through the toughest of times. Reeve stated, "It may be an accomplishment to fly solo, but there's a great deal more satisfaction in flying together." Dana echoed his words stating, "We really are a team, and that really is a gift."

The Reeves had taken an apparent negative and turned it into a positive. Reeve was asked on multiple occasions to intervene and help other people who had suffered spinal cord injuries, stroke, or paralysis. When they were at their emotional low points, he was there to lend encouragement and hope. Hope also motivated him. The Reeves set up the Christopher Reeve Paralysis Foundation in hopes of someday finding a cure for paralysis. They were on the front lines, raising awareness and needed research dollars, and progress continues to be made. Reeve once stated, "I can look at the future with genuine hope ... that there's useful work to be done."

A short time after Christopher Reeve died, Dana was hit with the tragic news that she had lung cancer, despite having never smoked. Just as Christopher's accident shined the light upon spinal cord injuries, Dana used her unwelcome news to raise public awareness about lung cancer. Her willingness to share her story saved lives. No doubt countless people around the world made lifestyle changes to reduce their risks for developing cancer.

Kryptonite was the only thing that could slow down Superman. Christopher and Dana Reeve had taken seemingly desperate situations and turned them into opportunities to really help humanity. Thankfully there was no kryptonite in their world. Their human spirits could not be harnessed. Thankfully they chose to lasso the sunshine!

History is replete with individuals who find themselves in situations that require them to make the most primitive of choices – give up or survive. War, by the very nature of the beast, fosters an environment teeming with survival opportunities. Senator John McCain, who many recall as the straight-talking former Republican presidential contender against George W. Bush, is a genuine Vietnam War hero who faced his own survival choices. As a naval aviator, McCain was shot down over Vietnam in 1967. He was injured and placed in a prisoner of war camp. In the book he co-authored with Mark Salter, *Faith of My Fathers*, McCain recounts the unspeakable atrocities he and the other POWs endured. He was held prisoner for five and one-half years, two of those alone in solitary confinement. Most of his limbs were broken or shattered. He suffered dysentery and severe weight loss. The emotional torture could be far worse than the physical torture. McCain stated that solitary confinement "… crushes your spirit and weakens your resistance more effectively than any other form of mistreatment."

McCain's story of survival is made even more inspirational because he did not have to suffer as he did. Early in his captivity he was offered his freedom. His father was a high-ranking Navy admiral, as was his grandfather before him. The North Vietnamese government intended to offer McCain his freedom as a ploy to embarrass the United States government. McCain, however, adhering to the Code of Conduct and a sense of honor he acquired from his family, refused. The Code of Conduct obliged a prisoner not to accept release earlier than others who may have been held captive longer. His refusal sealed his fate of enduring the cruelties of the POW camp for the next five years.

In the preface of McCain's memoir, he recounts the words written by Victor Frankel, a survivor of the concentration camp at Auschwitz. He wrote, "Everything can be taken from man but one thing: the last of human freedoms – to choose one's own attitude in any given set of circumstances, to choose one's own way." In essence, this is what lassoing the sunshine is all about. It is about making a choice in how one will respond to a given situation. It is about capturing the brighter side.

Men like John McCain and his fellow prisoners suffered through and endured terrible acts of inhumanity from their enemies. They were, however, unlike many of their unfortunate comrades, still alive. Through the blessings of life itself and their struggles to sustain it, they held on to a hope that they would perhaps live to enjoy a time yet to come. That seemed better than the alternative of not being alive to have that hope at all.

Speaking of hope, let me tell you about the hope a little boy named Hunter gives the world. As I was making mental notes to myself about what or whom to include in this book, I was inspired by the story of Hunter Kelly and his family. Hunter is the young child of the former Buffalo Bills quarterback great Jim Kelly and his wife, Jill. Hunter suffers from a rare condition known as Krabbe Leukodystrophy. Hunter was born with this condition and has required total assistance for his care ever since. Krabbe Leukodystrophy is a genetic neurological degenerative disorder that adversely affects the central and peripheral nervous systems. Children with this disease lack an enzyme that is essential to make something called myelin. Myelin acts as a protective covering for the nerve cells in the body. A lack of the enzyme causes a build-up of toxic substances that damage the nervous system. It has a devastating effect on the body. Children lose the ability to use their muscles and limbs, to talk, to swallow and eat, and even require assistance for breathing. Hunter's care is a twenty-four hour, seven-days-a-week endeavor. Most children afflicted with this disease do not live past two years of life. Hunter is now age seven and continues to inspire and provide hope for other children and families confronted with this illness throughout the world.

The Kellys have devoted all of their efforts towards helping their son overcome this great obstacle, as well as helping other families facing similar challenges. They have formed the Hunter's Hope Foundation to raise awareness, to provide support, and to raise needed funds in their fight for a cure. The key to fight this terrible disease is early detection. Umbilical cord blood and bone marrow transplants have proven effective in several newborns in preventing the development of the illness. It must be detected early, however, and herein lies a problem. Currently Krabbe and other leukodystrophies are not part of routine newborn screening tests. The Kellys and the Hunter's Hope Foundation are working to change this.

The fight against such a disease is a daily one, but thankfully Hunter is a tough little boy. In Jim Kelly's pro football Hall of Fame acceptance speech in August, 2002, he stated, "It has been well written throughout my career that toughness is my trademark. Well, the toughest person I've ever met in my life is my hero, my soldier, my son, Hunter. I love you, buddy." On the Kellys' web site for Hunter's Hope, they relate his accomplishments and the joys they share along the way. They are thankful for his accomplishments. They are thankful for him and all they learn from him. They state, "Hunter Kelly is the best example of everything that is important in life. He is also the best teacher. He continues to teach all of us the great value in hardships and suffering and the treasures found through trials and tribulations."

In their struggles the Kellys have found triumphs. Their faith seems to have been a great asset. On their website, they speak of prayer and of miracles. Hunter is their miracle. Prominently displayed on their opening web page is a verse from the Bible, Jeremiah 29:11: "For I know the plan I have for you," declares the Lord, "plans to prosper you and not to harm you, plans to give you hope, and a future." They have great hope for Hunter, and great hope of helping to prevent this disease in other children. They have hope for a future free of leukodystrophies – Hunter's Hope.

Just as Jim Kelly left a lasting impression with his eloquent words about Hunter during his Hall of Fame acceptance speech, another great sports legend inspired countless others with his words as well. The late basketball coach of the North Carolina State Wolfpack, Jim Valvano, both in the way he lived his life, and in the way he approached his imminent death, illustrated a lesson for us all in how to lasso the sunshine.

35

Coach Valvano will always be remembered for leading his North Carolina State team to the 1983 NCAA Men's Basketball Championship title. He was widely regarded in athletic circles as a coach with incredible zeal. His enthusiasm was contagious. He always seemed to be high on life and those around him seemed to always feel better in his presence. Many have credited his enthusiastic style, combined with his pure love of the game and love of his players, for his success.

From the time he was a young teenager, he had set a goal for himself of playing college basketball, coaching college basketball, and subsequently winning a NCAA division I title. He pictured it in his mind and even wrote it on an index card that he then carried in his wallet for many years. Such a positive mental attitude and vision of success was reflected in his players. We know this because no team has ever won (nor will any team ever win) a national title in any sport without first believing it could. Valvano believed it would happen and he convinced his players they could make it happen. Confidence in his players, his coaching strategies, and himself was the foundation upon which he built a national championship and took N.C. State and Jim Valvano to national prominence.

The characteristics that took Coach Valvano to the pinnacle of coaching would eventually serve him well in his struggles against the toughest competitor anyone can face – cancer. No one would have thought less of Coach Valvano if, when faced with the finality of terminal cancer, he would have quietly faded into the background to live out his last days. Not Jim Valvano. He unselfishly allowed strangers to share in his pain, his suffering, and his physical demise in hopes of helping others. He wanted to call attention to the scourge cancer of all types inflicts upon its victims and their loved ones. By publicly sharing his struggles, he hoped to one day prevent the suffering of others. He started, along with ESPN, the "V" Foundation for Cancer Research, which to this day has raised approximately thirty million dollars for cancer research. The goal is an eventual cure to this horrible disease.

Coach Valvano announced the inception of the "V" Foundation while accepting the Arthur Ashe Award at the ESPN Espy Awards. In a very emotional and often quoted speech, he stated, "Never give up, don't ever give up!" He knew his days were numbered, but thought his time could be best utilized encouraging others. Coach Valvano once commented that there were ". . . 86,400 seconds in a day," and he did not want to waste any of them. He wanted to make every second count, even when his seconds were limited. He deflected the focus away from his achievements as an individual, focusing instead on the global hurdles of millions facing cancer. His selfless acts and memorable acceptance speech continue to inspire countless individuals in their own daily struggles.

Even at a time when most people would be feeling sorry for themselves, grieving their impending early demise, Coach Jim Valvano found a way to lasso the sunshine, to find the brighter side of an admittedly dim situation. Such was his nature. Such was his approach to life. And such was the legacy he leaves behind.

One need not be a celebrity to inspire others. Being in the business of doctoring, I witness first-hand the triumphs and struggles and sometimes life-altering events in my patients' lives. Some events are beautiful miracles – the birth of a baby, a child with cochlear (ear) problems hearing for the first time what she had been missing, a grandmother walking pain-free after a knee replacement surgery, or a transplant recipient given a new lease on life. Some events are quite tragic – a young child requiring chemotherapy for cancer, a seemingly content person committing suicide, or a young person's life cut tragically short by an auto accident. Whether miracles or tragedies, I am constantly amazed how people cope with the challenges they encounter.

One of my patients, Mildred Fix, is a delightful, older lady who goes to my church. She recently suffered a major stroke that left her paralyzed on one side of her body. She is residing in a rehabilitation center, working with physical therapy; but as time passes, her hopes of regaining meaningful function of her affected limbs become more remote.

Fortunately, her cognitive skills remain intact, and as her friends, we as a congregation are privileged to learn from her wisdom. She shared with our pastor her view of her predicament. She understandably gets frustrated and down at times, but derives strength from her faith in God. She said to our pastor, "Every day I wake up and see the sun rising, and I think this is the day the Lord hath made, and I rejoice in it." Her spiritual beliefs allow her to overcome her physical ailments. That is what keeps her going, and that is what inspires the rest of us who are fortunate enough to know her.

The rising sun is a daily reminder to Mildred of her faith, and her faith helps her focus on all that she still has and enjoys. Her faith helps her focus on the brighter side.

# Climb to the Mountaintop, Then Ask for a Ladder

Once you have mastered the art of lassoing the sunshine, do not stop there. Apply those principles to other challenges you may encounter in your daily life. Cast your lasso at other objectives and make those a reality as well. You see, once you have lassoed the sunshine and captured the brighter side of life, you will then be operating from a perspective of optimism. Such optimism will undoubtedly flow forth from all aspects of your life. That optimism can even become contagious and positively impact those who have the good fortune of being in your presence. Optimism is a substrate for confidence, and confidence in turn breeds success.

Think about all of the successful people you have encountered in your life. How many of these people are pessimistic? How many of these people focus on the negatives? How many lack confidence? The fact is that most successful individuals possess a certain optimism and positive attitude about their goals and their ability to achieve those goals. One must not forget, however, that optimism and confidence alone are not enough to achieve success. Those traits coupled with hard work and focus are necessary ingredients. Hard work without focus could amount to wasted time and energy. Imagine a basketball player practicing his free throws. He will not get better if he is not focused on the task at hand. I have heard many coaches say practice does *not* make perfect; perfect practice makes perfect. Legendary Texas Tech Red Raiders basketball coach Bob Knight once commented in an ESPN interview that concentration was a key element to practice. He should know. He is a three-time NCAA national champion as a coach and one of the winningest coaches in the history of the sport. Be optimistic, have confidence, focus, and work hard – a recipe for success.

I am constantly amazed by those who seem to have it all, yet continue to strive for improvement. Tiger Woods, the golfing phenom of recent years, spoke in a television interview and discussed how he completely revamped his swing after one of the most lopsided, record-setting victories in the history of the Masters golf tournament. Why would the premier, number one rated golfer in the world, seemingly on the top of his game, abandon the swing that brought him championship after championship? He changed because he knew he could be even better.

Bill Gates, founder of Microsoft, is by all accounts one of the world's most successful businessmen. His innovation has changed our lives and brought him a financial portfolio many nations would envy. No one could blame him if he chose to quit working, travel the world, spend time with his numerous and very generous philanthropic endeavors, or just do anything else he wanted. He continues, however, to produce cutting edge computer programming and technology, striving to set the standard in the industry. He, like Tiger Woods, possesses and demonstrates that intangible trait of the human spirit that encourages one to reach the pinnacle of their chosen endeavors. They represent the ones who climb Mount Everest, reach the summit, and then ask for a ladder to go even higher.

When you get to the top of the mountain, do not get over-confident. While lassoing the sunshine and applying its principles of an optimistic outlook and confidence may have gotten you to the peak, dangers lurk. Never underestimate the power of the sun. Cling tightly to all of the positive aspects the sun offers, but be wary. One of the biggest mistakes we humans make is underestimating the power of the sun's rays. At any given moment, somewhere in the world, someone is getting sunburned. Whether on a sunny beach or high on the ski slopes, someone may have forgotten their sunscreen, or worse, may have made a conscious decision not to wear it. Some may have applied their lotion, but used a SPF 4 instead of a SPF 15 or 30. At least once most of us have experienced the consequences of such foolish behavior. We end up looking like a bright red lobster, whining with every little movement we make. Besides the obvious short-term effects, the outcome in the future may indeed be dire. The quest for the perfect tan may manifest itself as mere wrinkles in later life, or worse, skin cancer.

Just as the decision to ignore the power of the sun can have lasting consequences, the decision now to lasso the sunshine and apply its principles to our day-to-day activities can also have lasting effects.

When I was at the University of Illinois, I had the privilege of being able to walk-on the football team as a placekicker. It was not as easy as I had anticipated, however. Prior to arriving on campus in Champaign, Illinois, the special teams coach had told me I would have the opportunity to try out as a walk-on for the team. When I arrived in early August, I went for what I thought would be my try out, only to be told by the coach who promised me a shot at making the team that I would have to come back the following year. I was rather irritated by the whole affair, having spent my entire summer practicing in the evenings with a great friend of mine, Jeff Wright, who was kind enough to hold and retrieve balls for me. I thought about all of the long hours of practice and preparation. I was more than a little miffed to be told to come back next year after being promised a chance that fall. Despite pleading my case for just a five minute try out, I decided that I would be darned if he was going to ignore my kicking talents. Every day before the varsity came out to practice at Memorial Stadium, I would go out onto the artificial turf and kick, hoping to demonstrate to the special teams coach that I should, and deserved to be, a part of the Fighting Illini football team. One day one of the graduate assistant coaches was watching me and asked why I was not on the team. I explained to him the situation, and he stated he would tell the coaching staff at the meeting that night about me. He encouraged me to come back the following day (which I would have done anyway), and I did. Much to his dismay and mine, he was told by the other coaches to inform me to come back next year.

Discouraged but not deterred, I decided I would start staying on the field until the coaches kicked me off. The next day I continued to kick at the south end of the stadium field even while the other kickers and half of the team were warming up at the north end. The special teams coach came down and actually watched me for a few minutes. After successfully hitting fourteen out of fifteen attempts from forty and forty-five yards in his presence, he still told me to pick up my gear and come back next year. To me this fell under the definition of "unbelievable" in the dictionary.

Still perplexed and contemplating what my next course of action would be, an opportunity presented itself. Head coach Mike White came out of the locker room and strolled across the field at the opposite thirty-five yard line. I thought it could not hurt to kick just one more for Coach White to see. So I did. It was a fantastic forty-five yard field goal that split the uprights dead center, and could have carried for a fifty-five or sixty yarder. After witnessing only one kick, Coach White spoke briefly with the special teams coach. Shortly thereafter, as I was retrieving my football, the kicking coach approached me and told me to be at practice the next day.

I subsequently spent two years as one of several reserve kickers on the Fighting Illini team. It was two years filled with wonderful opportunities, wonderful people, and truly an experience of a lifetime just to be a part of a Big Ten college football program. Those two years brought lasting memories, friendships, and even more opportunities.

I was fortunate enough to be a part of the Fighting Illini football program during Coach John Mackovic's first two years at Illinois (he took over after Coach White left), and there exists no finer or classier coach in collegiate athletics. He played by the rules, never spoke negatively or went into tirades, commanded respect, and led by example. I am sure as a reserve walk-on placekicker he would not remember me, but I remember his approach to coaching. If I were ever in a position to be fortunate enough to coach young athletes, I hope I could do it even half as well as Coach Mackovic.

I had made a decision the day I was asked to be part of the team. I could have packed up and come back the next year, or I could have been persistent and hoped for the best. In a very real sense I lassoed the sunshine that day. I took my positive attitude and thought, "Nothing bad can come from kicking another ball for the head coach, and maybe something good can happen." Something good happened. The whole saga of just making the team and the way in which it happened gave me even more confidence for the future. It taught me the power of persistence. It reaffirmed to me that if one casts their lasso in hopes of capturing good things, it can and will happen. It is truly one of those life experiences that strengthened the attitudes I already had at the time, and in some ways contributed to the basis for this book. Work hard, create your own opportunities, think positively, and visualize positive outcomes. Such is the recipe for lassoing the sunshine and capturing the best life has to offer.

Even today I still reap the benefits of friendships made at the University of Illinois. Every December the Fighting Illini basketball team plays border rival, the Missouri Tigers, in what has become the hottest sporting event ticket in St. Louis. Yes, it is an even tougher ticket than the Rams, Cardinals, or Blues. My wife and I have not missed a game in the last thirteen years because of a good friend in a good position when it comes to obtaining tickets.

Just as underestimating the sun's power can lead to negative short-term ailments like sunburns and long-term ailments like skin cancer, lassoing the sun's positive attributes can lead to favorable outcomes. It gave me the opportunity years ago to see up close the workings of a Big Ten sports program, and even today look forward to watching the border battle between two of the nation's best basketball programs. I should note the sun does seem to shine more favorably upon the Illini, as Illinois holds the edge in wins over Missouri in the annual game.

# Think BIG

One lesson the world has taught us through the years – think BIG! We cannot be afraid to think big. Nothing substantial has ever been accomplished without first thinking about it. The sun is big. The sun's solar system is big. It may take a big lasso, but we can lasso it.

History is replete with individuals who were not afraid to think big. Heck, I have visions of sharing my "lasso the sunshine" message on Oprah's show. Oprah herself, simply by virtue of her enormous success, has to be a big thinker. Ben Franklin, Thomas Jefferson, Lewis and Clark, James Eads, Elizabeth Cady Stanton, Susan B. Anthony, Henry Ford, Thomas Edison, Albert Einstein, Dr. Martin Luther King, and Bill Gates are some more big thinkers. The transcontinental railroad, Panama Canal, Hoover Dam, Las Vegas strip, Golden Gate Bridge, St. Louis Gateway Arch, and the "Chunnel," connecting Great Britain to France under the English Channel are all the products of big thinking. Explorers, engineers, inventors, entrepreneurs, historical figures and builders have never been afraid to think big. These people were dreamers. They were not afraid to think big or to dream big.

Christopher Columbus did not want to just see the ocean, he wanted to see beyond the horizon. Lewis and Clark did not just pack for a picnic and overnight camp outing. They packed for a multi-year exploration to find a water route to the Pacific Ocean. President Kennedy not only wanted to look up and see the moon, he wanted man to walk on the moon. Engineers and builders are legendary for their lack of restraint in the big thinking arena. Need a way to get from England to France? We'll just build a tunnel under the English Channel. Trying to build a railroad line across a country and run into the Rocky Mountains? This is not a problem. We'll simply blast miles of tunnels through solid granite. Do you need to supply water to most of the southwestern United States? Perhaps we will just block a major river in the middle of nowhere and create the Hoover Dam. What about office space? Let's build the Empire State Building – at the height of the Great Depression – in less than a year. Do you need to cross the Mississippi River at St. Louis using late nineteenth century technology? Just ask Mr. James Eads to build you a bridge from Illinois to Missouri – a bridge that still carries automobiles and railcars across it to this day. And speaking of St. Louis, when we needed a monument to commemorate the opening and gateway to the West, a statue or historical marker did not seem to be enough. Instead, let's build a stainless steel arch six-hundred-thirty feet up into the sky!

Entrepreneurs are among the best known big thinkers. Henry Ford thought we all should have an automobile so he invented one and the assembly line to put it together. Ray Kroc thought customers would like his hamburgers. Customers, not just at the corner grill, but customers at every corner of the world. What kid does not love a Happy Meal from McDonald's? Mr. Bill Gates envisioned we would someday benefit from his computers and software. He envisioned a computer not just for use in big business, but also a personal computer in everyone's home and on everyone's desk in the country. His software helped me write this book.

Are you getting the picture? One has to think big to accomplish big things. I do not believe anything has ever been accomplished without it first being dreamed about in one's mind. Think big and dream big! Envision your goal and set out to reach it. It may not be easy, and in fact in most cases comes with varying degrees of sacrifice (people have died building bridges and dams). Failure is a natural stepping-stone on the pathway to success. Big thinkers embrace mistakes and alter plans that fail in an effort to improve the final outcome. So much is possible in our lives, and in many ways man's own preconceptions about the limits of those possibilities are our tallest hurdle to overcome. Remember, big plans may require a big lasso, but you can lasso that sunshine and make it yours!

# Live For the Moment

Just as the sun is the most important and central star in our solar system, so too is it important to focus on those people and things central in one's own life. Have you ever noticed when you go to an event such as a baseball game, it is not so much the event that matters, but that you shared it with someone who matters to you? The last St. Louis Cardinals baseball game I attended with my family was a great time, but I think it was the bottom of the fifth inning before I actually saw a pitch. With my five year-old, three year-old, and one year-old pointing out every ice cream, cotton candy, and peanut vendor in the stadium, it is hard to focus on the action on the field. In the grand scheme of things, that was just fine with me. The game was meaningless. The family time was rewarding.

Do not get me wrong. I certainly do feel at ease and a sense of serenity when I have the opportunity to be alone in my thoughts. I think everyone needs some "self" time to reflect on the world. I do some of my best thinking while jogging or just sitting outdoors taking in nature. The thought, however, of not having someone with whom to share life is a very sad and lonely one.

When I was a youngster, I had the good fortune of knowing all four of my grandparents very well. My maternal grandfather, Allen Milton, used to take me with him to work. He used to keep the oil wells maintained and pumping down the back roads of Southern Illinois. I vividly remember when I was about eight years-old stopping by the Kewpee Café in Benton, Illinois at six in the morning for Grandpa's breakfast and coffee, but, as I look back, probably more importantly for camaraderie. It was at this local greasy spoon that the blue collar men would gather before work, much like an after work watering hole, but this was for breakfast. Everyone knew my grandpa there, and he knew all of them. They called him "Slim," a nickname earned by his six feet, five inch tall, lanky frame. It did not matter what they ate for breakfast. It only mattered that they were there. It was a collection of various professions, but mostly coal miners. This was the era when coal was king in Southern Illinois. So many, including my other grandpa, relied upon it for their livelihoods. Now, unfortunately, the coal industry has left behind abandoned storefronts and only skeletons of abandoned mines as a reminder of the once thriving industry. The Kewpee Café held within its walls a collection of hard-working men just trying to make life better for their families and themselves.

Later that same day, after everyone had scattered throughout the area to earn their day's pay, we again encountered a similar congregation at lunch. This time it was at Burton's Café near Whittington. This appeared to be to the lunch hour what Kewpee's was to the breakfast hour. Again, a good place to fill one's tummy, but more importantly a place to fulfill one's sense of belonging. Kewpee's, Burton's, and undoubtedly countless other establishments across our great land provide a more important service than serving food – they serve as a focal point for the community, and in small-town America that means everything.

At places like these one could not only get a great stack of pancakes and eggs "sunny-side up," or some of Burton's famous white custard pie, one could get a friendly "hello" and a group of people that when they asked, "How are you doing?", actually cared about your answer. We need more places like Kewpee's and Burton's.

I recall while spending one day on oil well rounds we were driving the back roads of Franklin County between Buckner and Valier (at one time two thriving coal mining towns). As we approached an oncoming pick-up we both slowed and stopped – right there in the middle of the road. Granted, it was a backcountry, little traveled road, but it was still right in the middle of the road. My grandpa and this nice gentleman talked for about five minutes then we proceeded on our way. As we drove off, Grandpa said to me, "You know, Bobby, life wouldn't be worth living if it weren't for family and friends." My grandpa was no doubt a very enlightened man, and I was privileged to know him and share so many great times with him before he died.

My paternal grandpa, George "Windy" Farmer, from the aforementioned town of Valier, was also a source of enlightenment. He acquired the nickname, "Windy," because of his propensity to be full of hot air, people never knowing for sure whether to believe his tales or not. I recall when I was about sixteen years old, a few months prior to his death, he shared a most unexpected moment with me. I was telling him goodbye after a visit at his house and he asked me why I never said, "I love you," to him. This was quite unexpected for two reasons: he had never really said that to me, and it was coming from a man who was a "man's man." He had spent roughly fifty years in the coalmines of Southern Illinois. He could fix and do just about anything. He was seemingly invincible. He had always kept any emotions away from public view. He was the last person I expected to give me a lesson in love. But he did. He told me if I love someone I should tell them. He told me it was important that they know how I feel. As a sixteen year-old "man's man" myself, this caught me off guard and admittedly left me a little embarrassed. I never forgot this brief, private moment shared with my grandpa. A conversation that lasted mere seconds has given me a lifetime of guidance.

Cherish your time spent with family and friends. Cherish your memories of those now gone. My uncle, Carl Willis, shared with me the lessons life taught him after his wife (and my aunt) Sharon died of breast cancer at the young age of thirty-nine, leaving behind Carl and their two young children, my cousins Chris and Shari. My Aunt Sharon had been sick for quite some time, and her death was not something that took anyone by surprise. When someone dies at such a young age, however, it is never easy nor can one ever be totally prepared for the reality that they are actually gone. Sharon knew she was dying and had Carl bring their children to her hours prior to her death. Her last words to them, "I love you," are etched in Carl's memory and something that to this day are a vivid reminder of the wonderful wife, mother, and person she was.

Sharon, even in the weeks and months prior to her death, spent a great deal of her time focusing on others. She was an instructor in the Library Science Department at the University of Missouri, amongst the tops in her field, and even insisted on teaching her students via teleconference from bed only three weeks before she died. She and Carl took the kids on a canoe float trip in her final months, knowing she may not be able to in the future. She knew her prognosis was poor, but she kept her hope. She made a point of keeping all of their baby furniture and supplies, hoping to beat the cancer and someday have another child. Unfortunately, she lost her fight with cancer, but her spirit lives on in those whose lives she touched. Twenty years posthumously she was honored by the American Library Association for outstanding contributions to her field.

The day Sharon died a friend visited her in the hospital. Sharon deflected questions about her own welfare, instead choosing to talk about her friend's recent vacation. Right up to her death it was never about her. She was thankful for the time she had on this earth, and never appeared bitter that she had to leave it so soon. She truly sought the bright side... and found it, both during her time on earth, and most certainly in heaven.

The day following Sharon's death Carl sat down with his children in an attempt to explain to them what had happened to Mommy. They were ages six and nine, and understandably their view of the situation was somewhat different than the perspective brought to the table by Carl. After explaining the many implications for the future that Sharon's death would bring to their lives, each had a simple question. Chris wanted to know who would sew buttons back onto his shirts or fix holes in his pants. Shari inquired, "Who will make the chocolate cakes?" At first glance such questions would appear to show poor insight into the true meanings of the situation – at least as we adults tend to analyze things. But in reality, perhaps these questions point to a truth that only children in their innocence and mostly unskewed view of the world provide; that is, what is important to us today, right now?

No one knows how long we will be here or when the Man upstairs may call us home. We should live for the moment realizing yesterday is gone and tomorrow may never get here. These children were not thinking of next week or next year or even of the next decade. They were interested in today. In Coach John Wooden's book written with Steve Jamison, *Wooden – A Lifetime of Observations and Reflections On and Off the Court*, Wooden reflects:

"Too often we get distracted by what is outside our control. You can't do anything about yesterday. The door to the past has been shut and the key thrown away. You can do nothing about tomorrow. It is yet to come. However, tomorrow is in large part determined by what you do today. So make today a masterpiece. You have control over that."

My Aunt Sharon tried to live each day the best she could, her days cut tragically short by breast cancer. My Uncle Carl has lived each day since, doing the best he could in a difficult situation. He said Sharon's death made him a better parent. He had to become father and mother to his two young children. Sharon made the best of her final days, teaching right up until the end, and her family has gone on to make the best of their days.

Coach Wooden, deemed by many to be the most successful coach in NCAA basketball history, encourages us to focus on today. When Sharon died, the following day her children were focused on the problems of that day (such as who will mend the clothes). As the sun rises each day to bring new challenges, so too must we rise with it. Live for the moment. Live for today; an important lesson to help us lasso the sunshine whether brought to us through the words of a Hall of Fame basketball coach or the innocent eyes of a child.

# Rain, Rain, Go Away

No news is good news. Really, it is. Try it sometime. We recently enjoyed a family vacation to Destin, Florida. Some very good friends of ours graciously allow us the use of their condominium located right on the beach. It is a great time for the kids to build sandcastles and collect seashells – simple joys that in the grand scheme of life may seem incidental, but in truth are very important. No time is ever wasted sharing in happiness and discovery with your children.

We spent an entire week with no televisions, newspapers, or radios. We were on a news hiatus, and when we returned home, the world had not ended. I made only one exception, and that was to watch the Chicago Cubs in the National League Playoffs. Having attended the University of Illinois for four years, I had the poor misfortune of being barraged by the unbridled enthusiasm of large numbers of Cubs and Bears fans to the point of nausea. Thus, any chance I have to see the Cubs teeter on the edge of success, only to slip back down the mountain is enjoyable (just ask any Cardinals fan and you will find they agree with me). If you think about it, Cubs fans have to be some of the best lassoers of the sunshine around. They have to be, or life would get pretty desperate.

Have you ever noticed how sad the news can be? War, murders, layoffs, corruption, scandal – not too much of it is very uplifting. Bombarded by bad news day after day, hour after hour, on every twenty-four hour cable news station that exists, one may find it difficult to lasso the sunshine. It is as if a perpetual cloud has blocked the light of the sun, only occasionally peeking out with a bit of good news for a transient reminder that it is still there. It would be easy to get down watching this on a daily basis. But remember two things. First, it is news because it still is not the norm. When war, murder, robbery, and child abduction stop making the news, then we really will be in trouble. Second, one can always turn it off.

Believe me – if you turn off the news you are not missing anything. Does anyone really think they would miss something meaningful or important if, for instance, they missed their congressman's or senator's latest rantings about how to cure the economy, education, or healthcare. I would argue one is better for not having been exposed to such horse manure. Most of them, in either party, do not even believe their own statements, but know what to say to play to their constituents. No principles, no problem; just as long as they can get re-elected, pad their pensions, and ensure their continual supply of special interest money, they have accomplished their goal. So, by avoiding the news periodically, one can avoid the perpetual cloud blocking the sun. With the needless clouds out of the way, it is much easier to focus on all that is good in the world and lasso the sunshine.

# Nature's Screenplay

One thing I have noticed about nature is it always seems to teach me something about life. Not only does the sun provide us with examples, but so many other aspects of nature provide guidance as well, if we just take the time to observe. Observe, not just by looking and seeing, but also by listening and feeling.

During a recent family vacation to Destin, Florida, I was getting all of the usual warm fuzzies watching the tiny footprints my children were leaving in the sand. But just as quickly as they were there, the gentle ebb and flow of the tide washed the footprints away, almost as if the simple stroke of an artist's brush had touched the sand. It struck me that for many of the seemingly endless little stresses we all encounter in our lives, perhaps nature has the right idea. The beach sustains a little blemish and the tide is there to quickly wash it away to restore the surface. In the big scheme of things, we should approach many of the little stresses we encounter as little blemishes on our beach of life. Just brush the little stresses aside, not focusing on them or giving them much attention – no more than a brief blemish that comes and goes. Look to the sand and sea to wash your worries away, and look to the sky to lasso the sunshine.

The constant crashing of waves told me that nature had even more to teach me. I have decided that so much that occurs in nature is truly a metaphor for life. As the tide came and went, and the never-ending procession of crashing waves filled the background sounds of the beach, I was inspired by nature's persistence. It must get tiring to constantly attempt to make progress in one direction, only to be halted by this thing called land. But the waves and the water never tire. The tide reaches its furthest point, turns around, and heads back out to sea, only to someday try it again. There are no signs here of discouragement or quitting – only persistence. In fact, even as I was writing this passage, I peaked out to the beach to see the waves lapping at the edge of our sandcastle pails and beach towels. Only thirty minutes earlier they were safely away from the tide's grasp.

As I gazed out to the horizon nature continued to teach me. At the point in the distance where the water meets the sky I could not help but think of hope and faith -- hope that there is something more beyond the horizon, and faith that indeed there is. Again, nature was speaking. Hope is basically a longing for something to be. Faith, at its essence, is a belief in something of which we have no confirmation. I wondered what the first human to view the ocean must have thought. I put myself in his position. As I looked to the horizon, I certainly hoped there was something beyond the "edge of the world." Via faith, I just knew there was.

The beach is a teacher. So many elements combine to give one the whole beach experience. Broken down to its most basic components, the beach is nothing more than a seemingly infinite number of individual sand particles. What can one little, almost microscopic sand particle teach us? We are all well-versed in the manner in which a single particle of sand can lead an oyster to give birth to a pearl. We know how irritating sand can be in our swimsuits, hair, shoes, etc. But sand also teaches us about teamwork. One tiny particle of sand can be an irritant, both to people and oysters. Infinite particles of sand, however, make a beach. That irritant by itself all of the sudden in mass becomes a vacation destination. I wonder what people the world over could do by working together.

I normally would not spend my time writing while on a family vacation, but while my wife was building sandcastles with my two oldest children, I was in our beachfront room with our one year-old while she napped. I took advantage of the time to reflect and write. As I was writing, several beautiful sailboats passed by on their way to who knows where. If my guess was correct, the captain and crew probably did not know for sure either. I imagined them to be Jimmy Buffett types whose destination is happiness, and where every port of call along the way is filled with relaxation, good times, and good "spirits."

I imagine one must be fairly patient to be a sailor. If there is no wind (or no motor) you drift. When there is wind, you have to take what nature gives you and make the best of it. I think what I admire, though, is how the sailor can take ever-changing conditions and wind directions, and still seem to get to their intended destination. They are the ultimate adapters. They are able to tack and first go east to eventually go west. I unfortunately was unfamiliar with this concept on the first day of our honeymoon in Jamaica. After a five-minute sailing seminar, my bride and I headed for the open sea in a two-person sailboat they offer at these all-inclusive beach resorts. I was the captain of my ship with my first soul mate at my side. The refreshing aroma of the salty sea breezes was filling my airways – I was the captain; I was the man! I was the man all the way up until the point when we started drifting towards a rock jetty and I realized I had not the slightest clue about what I was doing. I had not paid proper attention during the "drifting uncontrollably towards a rock jetty" section of the sailing course. We were eventually "rescued" ten feet from the perilous, jagged jetty by two of the resort staff. One of them boarded our vessel and sailed us safely back to shore, but not before heading further out to sea first. Ahh – the art of tacking. Perhaps this is why I can fully appreciate our modern day Christopher Columbi (plural of Columbus) who choose to tackle the open sea. They take a set of circumstances and adapt to reach a goal – certainly a quality useful in most of life's endeavors. Even something nature gives us that we cannot see, such as the ocean winds, can still teach us a lesson applicable for life.

During our Florida vacation we were blessed with wonderful weather – seventy-five degree, mostly sunny-sky days provided the backdrop for the brilliant hues of turquoise, blue, and green that all seamlessly melded together as we looked out to the Gulf of

Mexico.  The beaches of Destin, Florida are some of the most powdery, whitest, cleanest, and family-friendly beaches one could hope to visit.  The sun shone brightly most days with occasional clouds passing overhead.  There were not enough clouds to foil the sun's rays, but just enough to unleash the imagination.  I saw ships sailing across the sky, the puffy cumulus clouds doubling as large sails.  At one moment I sailed with Blackbeard and his pirate crew, swinging our cannons toward the approaching enemy ship.  The next moment I was enjoying cotton candy at a St. Louis Cardinals baseball game, the sugary strands of candy disappearing on my palate just as quickly as the clouds transformed shapes.  I was harkened out of my nature-induced trance by passing pelicans, soaring in formation, surveying the shallows in search of a quick snack.  The first time I saw a pelican was during a family vacation as a child in Daytona Beach, Florida.  I had just learned about dinosaurs in our studies of prehistoric times, and I was convinced I was witnessing the flight of a pterodactyl.  Even to this day, I cannot help but be reminded of the many family vacations we enjoyed when I was a kid, and everything is right with the world.

Sitting and writing on the balcony that afternoon, I had front-row seats to the best theater nature had to offer.  Looking out to sea, about an hour before sunset, the sun can seem at its brightest.  The sun and its linear reflection across the water can be blinding.  Nature seems to be marking the way for those who take notice.

The reflection across the undulating water's surface, like a kaleidoscope of brilliant, shimmering diamonds, leads directly to its source. Perhaps this is nature's attempt to say "follow the path to the brighter side." Perhaps nature is calling us to lasso the sunshine.

At sunset that evening we took advantage of the setting sun to take some family photos. It was my attempt to merge what I see as the beauty of my family with the beauty of nature. The Destin sunset in early October provides the perfect backdrop to complement the most beautiful family for which a guy could ever hope. Palm trees, white sand, sailboats, seagulls, pelicans, and white-capped waves supply ample mood to enhance any sunset photography. The sun's rays are refracted by the atmosphere to produce a color and light show even the most skilled artist cannot re-create (although Terry Redlin, a wonderful artist who weaves nature's lighting into almost all of his works comes as close as any mortal could). Combine nature's beauty and my family's smiles, and one has a "can't miss" photo opportunity.

Year after year I am lucky enough to place these photographs on my desk at work to remind me of such serene and happy moments. Looking back at the pictures of that day, they provide a sort of visual onomatopoeia, the sights conjuring up the unique sounds of nature: the crash and roar of the surf, the flapping of kites in the wind, and the call of seagulls in the distance. In any event, that year's photography attempts were the same as previous years. They again provided me with pictures that I look at on a daily basis to remind me just how truly blessed I am.

On the particular evening we were taking our family photos, I noticed a man standing with a woman on the beach. He dropped to his knees and looked up to her in what appeared to be a full, all-out proposal mode. I had already placed the lens cover back on my camera and missed the perfect "romance" photo. I did, however, manage to get a shot of the couple's subsequent embrace and kiss with the sun setting in the background. Oh, how many proposals the setting sun has surely witnessed! Risking intrusion, I went down to ask the couple if they would like a copy of the photograph capturing that magic moment. The gentleman had gone back inside briefly, and the woman informed me she had actually just received a ring from her husband celebrating their twenty-fifth wedding anniversary. I told her I hoped I was not intruding on their special moment, and she related how happy she would be to have a copy of their embrace. In fact, she said another young couple had been walking the beach a short time earlier, and they were lacking a camera. The twenty-fifth anniversary couple used their camera to take a picture of the other young couple and planned to send it to them as well. It was a classic case of one good deed leads to another. This time all of the participants were brought to the same locale by one central actor – the sun.

All who had gathered at the beach that night were in search of that seemingly intangible moment when the sun gently kisses the sea. It is an instant when we are so engrossed in the moment, so enthralled by the beauty, that all else is forgotten, and everything in the world is in its proper place. It is a moment, ever so transient, that leaves a lasting impression on all who witness it. Those who have seen it once long to see it again, as testified to by the throngs of people walking the beach or standing attentive on balconies, many armed with camera and film to capture the moment. Sunset is a moment of serenity, comfort, and relaxation. It is a moment of contentment and happiness. It is a moment that stirs all of those human emotions that make us feel good inside. It is a time that at the exact same instant, someone far away standing on a beach looking to the east is experiencing a beautiful sunrise as a start to their day. The sun is Mother Nature's way of tucking part of the world in to sleep, and gently nudging the rest of the world to arise for a new day, all at the same time. The sun – strive to accept what it has to offer and what it wants to teach us. The sun – lasso it and find the brighter side of life!

The sun, as we know, is the main character in our Broadway production of life, but there are also many supporting members to our ensemble cast. One does not have to be at a beach to be inspired by nature. Every natural environment has something to teach us. From the frozen polar ice caps to the hottest, driest, deserts, we can learn from nature.

Glaciers teach us persistence, moving inch by inch while leaving vast valleys in their wakes. Rivers, too, show persistence. One needs to look no further than the Grand Canyon to see the results of the relentless work of the Colorado River. The redwood trees of California remind us of stability and endurance. They have stood through centuries of forest fires and earthquakes. Old Faithful, the geyser in the geothermal fields of northwestern Wyoming, inspires us with its reliability. An entire tourist trade has been built around this "faithful" natural wonder. Volcanoes demonstrate the continued renewal of our planet. Though Mother Earth is aging, the molten lava provides renewal and replenishment. We are all aging, too, but should strive to remain young at heart. The aurora borealis, or Northern Lights, illuminates the darkness with a dazzling array of colors. We also should strive to find light in times of darkness. When it comes to nature's Broadway stage show, the sun wins the award for best actor, but so many other natural elements get the nod for best supporting actor. Take a page from nature's screenplay and start rehearsing the lines. After a few readings you will be on your way to lassoing the sunshine!

# Why the Rooster Crows At Dawn

The rooster could very easily be the most optimistic of all of God's creatures. Every single day he awakens at dawn and crows in all of his glory. Every single day! Let's say that one more time – every single day! He crows despite other potential problems in his life. He must be wary of the sly old fox and other predators, never knowing when one could sneak up behind him. Worse yet, even his owner is a potential enemy. In the song, "She'll Be Coming Around the Mountain," we all know it is the farmer who "kills that old red rooster" to make chicken and dumplings – Chop! Chop!

Given that knowledge, why does the rooster crow at dawn? That is a tough question, and no one may ever know the true answer to it. The importance of this, though, is not really in the why, but in the simple fact that he does. When the sun rises in the east, the rooster welcomes it with a hearty crow.

If we could apply the principle of the rooster in our lives, we would awaken each morning and welcome the new day in a positive fashion. "Getting off on the right foot," or rolling out on the "right" side of the bed are old clichés, but the old sayings can be timeless in their wisdom as they relate to our daily approach to life.

There exist many others of God's creatures to teach us a thing or two about life. The busy beaver, through his industriousness, can dam up creeks and rivers. Beavers can work tirelessly to finish the job, sometimes dropping trees large enough to make a lumberjack proud. If man could harness the beaver's energy and work ethic on a proportional pound for pound basis, just think how much we could accomplish.

Salmon every year decide it is a good idea to swim upstream and in many cases against the rapids in order to carry on their species. One would think there has to be an easier way, but these fish are undeterred in their mission. They have one goal in mind and do not stop until the mission is accomplished – certainly an admirable trait.

The turtle and the snail certainly must be patient fellows. It sure takes them a long time to get where they are going, but they seem to get there. Our impatient society could learn a thing or two from these slow and steady creatures. At least they do not have to worry where they will stay each night – they carry their lodging with them.

Whether it be from the various environments of nature or the creatures that occupy those environments, all we need to do is just stop and look around. We can learn so much if we just pay attention. Mother Nature can help us lasso the sunshine and so much more!

# My Daily
# Dose of Sunshine

There are several events that happen every day in my life that make it very simple for me to lasso the sunshine. I believe most people probably have a routine each morning of waking up and preparing for their day. I would venture to guess that for many that routine is fairly repetitive and maybe even mundane. Such is not the case for me. Repetitive yes, mundane no. Every morning after I kiss my wife and children goodbye (they are all usually still asleep as I leave quite early to make my hospital rounds), I drive the same route to the hospital. During the quiet, approximately ten to fifteen minute drive, I have the opportunity to do two things that are very important to me: pray to God and pay homage to the symbol of my country.

Just three minutes from my home on the way to the hospital stands a cell phone tower disguised as a flagpole. In fact, if I had not been informed that it was a cell phone tower, I would have always thought it an attempt to have one of the Midwest's tallest flagpoles. In any event, the flag that furls in the wind from this pole is proportionally large as well. The flag waves proudly in front of a junior high school on one of the highest points in the county and is visible for many miles in many directions. Against the backdrop of the morning sky at sunrise, with all of the vibrant shades of pinks and purples and oranges and blues, it is truly an inspiring sight. The sun usually accompanies me on my morning trek to work, which, given the theme of these writings, is entirely appropriate. The daily sight of Old Glory reminds me how thankful and blessed I am to be an American. Some may find such remarks to have a ring of arrogance, that somehow Americans are better than others. I do not believe that any one group of people is in any way better than another group of people. I do, however, believe we, as Americans, are indeed luckier and more blessed than other peoples. Despite her many flaws, and the Lord knows she has them, America is the greatest country on the planet, but only because the Man upstairs says so. And that leads me to another of my daily rituals – prayer.

Prayer, to me and many others, is very important. I pray every day during my "quiet time," that fifteen-minute drive to work. I kiss my family goodbye, get in the car, drive by the Stars and Stripes, and then begin my daily prayer. I thank God for my life, my faith in Christ, my family, my country, and my place in the world (just to name a few things – one can talk about a lot of things with God in fifteen minutes). I ask for his guidance throughout the day, and I thank him for all of the countless blessings he has given me. I once read on one of Garth Brooks' album covers that it is through God's grace that we enjoy the things that we do not deserve, and it is through God's mercy that we do not get the things that we do deserve. Obviously Mr. Brooks was blessed with not only great musical talent, but also great wisdom.

I find my morning routine to be a truly soothing and peaceful way to start the day. I believe it allows me to be in the frame of mind to better handle any challenges or hurdles that may pop up throughout the course of the day. My faith and my appreciation for all that is so wonderful in my life provide me with a foundation to plant my feet before I cast my lasso. There is a memorable line in the classic Hollywood movie, "Cool Hand Luke," in which the prison warden asks the prisoner, Luke, portrayed by Paul Newman, "You got your mind right yet, boy?" My daily ritual of kissing my wife and children, staring in gratitude at the symbol of my country, and praying to God gets my mind right to tackle a new day. It allows me to start from a positive base, which subsequently allows me to feel good and project a more positive response to the upcoming day's events.

Although my days usually begin the same, and the general schedule leans toward a potentially monotonous routine, there are many seemingly small, usually very brief and transient events that make getting out of bed all worthwhile. I look forward to these happenings. It may be a few simple words a patient or colleague shares with me, or perhaps someone just telling me that they appreciate what I do. It is always nice to be appreciated. My Uncle Carl once told me that people like to feel that they are valued. It is a simple concept and may seem obvious, but as we go through our daily lives I think we sometimes forget. It does not take long to say to someone, "Thank you – thank you for what you do. I really appreciate and value what you do, and I appreciate and value you." These words, expressed with meaning and sincerity, can go a long way. Most of us respond to positive reinforcement. Telling people you appreciate them reinforces the behavior that made you appreciate them in the first place. Good old-fashioned etiquette does much to improve the workplace and the world.

There have been many times in my young career when I have become frustrated in my profession. There are days when no one seems appreciative. On the contrary, everyone seems demanding. People can be impatient and downright rude. Charts are piling up on my desk. Insurance companies are on the phone and want to know how my patient who just suffered a heart attack two days earlier could possibly still be in the hospital. My malpractice insurance premium arrives in the mail with a one-hundred percent increase over my previous year's rates, not because I am some quack physician who happens to get sued a lot, but because I chose to practice medicine where I grew up in perhaps one of the most litigious, politically corrupt, and ethically challenged counties in the United States. And all of this before lunch, that is, if I get time to eat lunch that day. So just as I am wondering why I went to medical school, or for that matter why I even got out of bed that day, one of my ninety year-old patients brings in a cake she has baked and tells my staff and me "thank you" for helping her through a tough time she experienced the week before. At that point I could not care less about all of the other distractions. She is happy and thankful and through her smile she has made me happy and thankful – happy to have patients like her who never fail to restore my belief that most people are good people, and thankful that God has allowed me to be a physician. No combination of rude people, unreasonable insurance reviewers, or ethically void political hacks can quell my patient's appreciation for me or my appreciation for her. People like her make it easy for me to lasso the sunshine.

Other little things that happen during my days make me smile. I think I became a family doctor primarily because I like to talk to people. I like to hear their stories. I enjoy hearing about the many varied and interesting events in my patients' lives. They tell me about their vacations, their families, and their jobs. Patients share the world with their doctor. They share their joys and their sorrows, their victories and their defeats, and their hopes and their dreams. It is a unique privilege to have people open a door to their lives and allow me to look inside. I have patients who are pararescue troopers, air-tanker refueler pilots, farmers, teachers, artists, computer specialists, authors, radio and television anchors, bankers, business executives, butchers, bakers, cartographers, historic guides, and school and university presidents. They are coal miners, coaches, war veterans, professional fisherman, pool sharks, cardiologists, radiologists, casino dealers, casino owners, marathon runners, Civil War re-enactors, thoroughbred owners, jockeys, professional golfers, professional bowlers, FBI agents, ATF agents, pharmacists, chefs, carpenters, bricklayers, podiatrists, pediatricians, pathologists, stockbrokers, stockcar racers, pastors, Christmas tree farmers, attorneys, nurses, therapists, housewives, veterinarians, wood carvers, obstetricians, microbiologists, restaurant owners, dentists, machinists, mechanics, Black Hawk helicopter pilots, and Banzai tree farmers. The list is seemingly endless. The people and personalities are as varied as their professions. They tell me their stories. They let me into their lives. They teach me and tell me things I did not know. I share events in my life with them. I like to talk as much as I like to listen (some of my friends would argue more so). It is these brief moments, these little windows into the worlds of my patients, which I look forward to. I truly receive more satisfaction talking with a grandmother about her grandchildren and plans for Christmas than I do treating her arthritic knee. I think sometimes the grandmother would also share that view. Every day my patients treat me to their stories, which create in mass a mosaic of life that no artist could re-create.

As I leave my office each day I look forward with great anticipation to going home to my family. No matter how hectic or busy the day, I know that home will be a bastion of happiness and relaxation. Just as I left my family with the early morning sunrise and all was right with the world, so too does the setting sun accompany me on the evening drive home (especially in the winter) and all is again right with the world. My wife and children have a way of making it easy to leave work at the office. As I have stated, my job is filled with countless rewards, but there are many stressors as well. These worries usually go out the door as I am going in the door of my home. My wife and kids all greet me with hugs and kisses and are genuinely excited to see Dad. Their smiles can light up a room. I will always remember one night I arrived home after a particularly long and stressful day at work. It was one of those days predominated by some rude people, irritating phone calls, useless triplicate paperwork, etc. My oldest child, Austin was about nine months old at the time. I walked in the house, he smiled and said, "Da-Da," with great enthusiasm, and all the problems of the day were immediately forgotten. That single moment put life into perspective. I told my wife, Christina, that every time he smiled it made me smile, and it even prompted a spontaneous outbreak of poetry that I wrote about him, which now hangs proudly in our kitchen accompanied by his picture. As we had our next two children, Alexis and then Ashleigh, I was further inspired and penned a poem unique to each of them as well. These, too, occupy a prominent place on our kitchen wall along with their pictures. In the following pages I share those poems, inspired by the wonder, innocence, and excitement that children bring into our lives. I also share a poem about my family as a whole. We sent the family poem out in our Christmas cards.

# A Child's Smile
Inspired by Austin

Every time you smile
You make me smile too,
For there's nothing better in the world
Than a smile that comes from you.

You never have to wonder
If your smile is sincere,
Because a smile from a child
Is just as it appears.

Your smile is contagious
And your laughter fills the room,
Soon everyone who's near to you
Will laugh and smile too.

Every time you smile
The world's a different place,
Every time you smile
All of my problems are erased.

If every day could start
With just a glimpse of your bright smile,
The world would be a better place
Because of a smile from a child.

## Reflections of Heaven
Inspired by Alexis

Reflections of Heaven
I see in your face,
No purer an image
No more perfect a place.

God's loving hands
Have surely left their mark
On his perfect creation,
A new life to embark.

Ten tiny fingers
And ten tiny toes,
How it all comes together
Only God truly knows.

Brought down from Heaven
Upon angel's wings,
The birth of a child
A miraculous scene.

With you in our lives
The world's fresh and new,
A small piece of Heaven
Arrived here with you.

Reflections of Heaven
I see in your eyes,
Truly we've won
God's greatest prize!

## My Angel
Inspired by Ashleigh

My very special angel
I hold you in my arms,
Your halo on my shoulder
Your wings against my heart.

No man could ever be
So very blessed as me,
I hold a piece of Heaven
So close against my cheek.

God sent another angel
To remind us of His love,
For every little child
A true gift from above.

The wonder and excitement
Of what the future holds,
The promise of a lifetime
Of long and happy roads.

My precious little angel
You'll grow as time goes by,
Soon you'll spread your wings
I can't wait to see you fly.

## My Family
Inspired by Love

What is most important
In this world to me?
The answer is quite simple –
It's my family.

God has truly blessed our home
And filled these walls with love.
He's sent along some angels
To watch us from above.

If I get distracted,
Caught up in job or wealth,
I must take a few steps back,
I must remind myself.

Life's not about the money,
The toys, the clothes, the cars.
It's all about the riches
You find within your heart.

So what is most important –
Of course, my family.
They are the very special people
Who make my life complete.

My wife and children are my heart and soul. As one can tell from my poetry, they inspire me. Sometimes I feel like God unleashes in my mind a kind of controlled mania. Thoughts spontaneously enter my mind like lightning striking from a clear sky. The previous poems are prime examples. I am so blessed to have the wife and children that I do. They are my daily dose of sunshine, and they make lassoing the sun a cakewalk!

# **Find Your Passion**

Lasso the sunshine, quite obviously, can have many different connotations. It can be about one's approach to life, its challenges, and its many ups and downs. It is about how we respond to those challenges. On another level, lassoing the sunshine can be about a passion in one's life, a focus for one's energies. Family and faith certainly stand firmly on the top rungs of my ladder. One's occupation may be high on that ladder, but unfortunately for many that is not the case. Hobbies, sports, music, clubs, books, and travel are examples of outlets in which many exert their time and efforts.

Sports have always played a large role in my life. To some, the idea of throwing a football, shooting a basketball, chasing a golf ball, etc. may seem a useless endeavor. For many, myself included, sports provide a framework to build discipline, confidence, character, heart, teamwork, and mental toughness. Sports are not for everyone, and many other avenues can be taken in life that will develop the same traits. My dad would always remind me that as kids growing up in a complicated world, we all need to find something from which we can derive self-esteem. For some children that is sports, for others it may be the band or choir, or perhaps the chess, science, or debate club. No matter what the focus of one's energies or passion may be, it is important to find one.

As I was growing up in middle-class America, I was blessed to have many dedicated teachers and coaches. In fact, it would be a much shorter list for me to enumerate the marginal teachers and coaches than it would be to list the many, many terrific instructors from whom I had the good fortune to learn.

My fifth-grade basketball coach, Jim Rosborg, taught me two very important lessons in life: teamwork and sportsmanship. My mom and dad and older brother, Alan, instilled these traits into me at an earlier age, but as my first coach in an organized school team sport, Mr. Rosborg built upon that foundation. Fifth-grade was the first year our school played basketball. Every kid got to play, but every kid had to play with teamwork. A standing rule was if you were on a fast break and a teammate was ahead of you down the court, even if it was only one foot, you had to pass it to him. Failure to do so resulted in a nice spot on the bench. It did not take long for us to realize he meant what he said. As a result, no group of fifth-graders anywhere has ever played so well together. We were a well-oiled machine. Teamwork led to winning, but winning is not important without sportsmanship. Coach Rosborg led by example, always exemplifying the highest degree of integrity. He did not tolerate poor attitudes, hot-dogging, or "trash talking." Because of our fifth-grade coach, I am confident all of my teammates and me are better people today. It is not surprising that Coach Rosborg is now a very successful and highly regarded district superintendent and statewide educational leader. He just recently was recognized by the State of Illinois as its Outstanding Superintendent of the Year.

My high school basketball coach, Jim Reynolds, also left a lasting impression. After practice one day I was talking to a teammate about how much potential I thought a particular college basketball player had. Coach interrupted me and said, "Farmer, do you know what potential is? Potential is ability sitting on its ass! Don't let anyone ever tell you that you've got potential. All that means is that you're not working hard enough and you're wasting your talents." He is right! I cannot watch a basketball game on television and hear a commentator remark on how much potential a player or team may have without thinking of Coach Reynolds and smiling.

As stated earlier, sports have played a major role in my life. My dad still likes to play my older brother and me in H-O-R-S-E in our backyard. When dad wins he likes to remind us boys that he is blind in one eye and has an arthritic wrist. He tells us an old guy like himself should not be able to still take two young whippersnappers in basketball. In my defense, it is not as bad as it sounds. My old man scored over twenty-four hundred points in his high school basketball career and once scored twenty-nine points in one quarter! My brother and I still like to go out and bang the tennis ball back and forth on occasion. My brother is a far, far better tennis player than me. I can play my absolute best and he still cleans my clock. I do not mind, though, as he brings out the best in my competitive side. Sports have provided me with a lifetime of memories, countless bonding opportunities with my family and friends, and a basis for development of self-esteem. I cannot tell you how many hours I spent playing pick-up basketball with one of my best friends, Jeff Wright, on his driveway. We played any time of the year, in the sweltering humid heat of summer to the bitter cold of winter. It kept us out of trouble, and made us better athletes, better people, and the best of friends. Jeff is now the head massage therapist for the St. Louis Blues (and I can still dominate him at hoops)!

My high school tennis coach, Mike Thompson, taught me a lasting lesson as well. My freshman year at Belleville East we had four "highly touted" freshmen – three of my good friends and me. Please remember, "highly touted" is a relative term. We had spent several summers playing tennis together, and two of us had older brothers who were standouts in their day. I know we thought we were good, but I also know I did not think we were *that* good. During one of our first team meetings, Coach Thompson told us he believed with hard work and dedication that we had a legitimate shot at the Illinois State Tennis Title over the course of the next four years. My first three seasons I am quite certain I did not share his optimistic attitude. By our senior year, however, as the season progressed, I began to believe it too. Under the right circumstances, peaking at the right time, we really could have a shot at the state title.

My doubles partner was my lifetime childhood friend, Robb Rickett. He was six-feet, six inches tall, the power forward and leading scorer on our basketball team (the best basketball player in a school of two-thousand-five-hundred students), and just an all-around good guy. Today he is a proud husband and father, and a very successful broker in Chicago. Together we peaked at the right time, the planets were aligned in our favor, and we managed to finish second in the Illinois State Tennis Tournament. I am certain the only reason that occurred was because Coach Thompson believed in his players and instilled that belief into us. It took four years, but he saturated our minds every practice and every match with positive thinking.

In Bob Valvano's biography of his brother, *The Gifts of Jimmy V*, he commented that Coach V. always attributed a person's success to the fact that somewhere in that person's life was someone else who believed in him. Coach Thompson believed in us. In four years I do not believe I ever saw him hit a tennis ball himself. He did not have to. Today he is in the Illinois High School Tennis Hall of Fame.

During my four wonderful years at the University of Illinois, I had the opportunity to witness the style of football coach John Mackovic. Coach Mackovic is one of the best in the business. Prior to his time at the University of Illinois, he was head coach at Wake Forest University and then the Kansas City Chiefs, turning them both into winning programs. In his first team meeting at the University of Illinois in the spring of 1988, Coach Mackovic made it clear he came to the University of Illinois for one reason: to win a national championship. In the team meeting room at Memorial

Stadium one wall pays homage to the 1983 Fighting Illini Rose Bowl team, a team that went 9-0 in the Big Ten. Mackovic pointed to the wall and told us any team that goes undefeated in the Big Ten and subsequently wins the Rose Bowl would be the undisputed National Champion. That would require defeating perennial powerhouses Michigan and Ohio State, and eventually the PAC-10 conference champion. Any team that could do that, he said, had claim to the title. (At that time the Big Ten always sent its conference champion to the Rose Bowl. Today, such is not always the case as the BCS rotates the national title game between four of the larger bowls, and the Big Ten representative may be sent to another bowl).

Coach Mackovic told us in order to achieve our goal of winning the Rose Bowl, we must first learn about our goal. Most of us had never been to California, much less the Rose Bowl. Mackovic's plan was simple – we learn about it so we can better appreciate what it is for which we are striving. Each week of the spring practice season Coach Mackovic planned to give several players questions about the history of the Rose Bowl to research and report back the following week to the team. Questions such as, "Who played in the first Rose Bowl?" and, "When did Illinois first reach the Rose Bowl?" One week after Coach had given out the first assignments to five different players, we reported to the team meeting room to hear the answers. The first player asked to give his response was a starting lineman from the previous year.

"I forgot to do it," he told Coach. Mackovic glared but did not yell or scream at the player. The room fell silent. Mackovic did not curse, nor did he throw things or go into a tirade. He simply went on to the next player for the response to the second question. One of the defensive backs was responsible for the answer to question number two. He answered correctly and even added some extraneous but interesting facts to boot. The team's response was evident, with an eruption of high-fives and excitement which was in stark contrast to deafening silence following the initial failed response. Mackovic took the opportunity to point out the difference in the team's reaction to the events that had just occurred. He looked at the lineman and said, "I asked you to do a simple assignment and you failed. How can I expect you to pull downline against Michigan in the fourth quarter when the game's on the line, when you can't even do something as simple as finding an answer to a question?" Mackovic went on to point out the defensive back had "done more than I asked of him – giving more information and going beyond the call." He pointed out the team's hushed response to failing one's assignment, and the team's enthusiastic response to completing one's assignment. The first is a recipe for failure and defeat, the latter a recipe for a national title. The lineman dropped from first string on the depth chart to the bottom of the chart and was relegated to the scout team for several weeks. Coach Mackovic very eloquently made his point, teaching a valuable lesson without ever raising his voice.    Such was Coach Mackovic's style.    He commanded respect, and he duly received it.

Sports are one of my passions.  They provide me with an outlet from the real world.  Whatever your passion, find it and follow it.  The secondary benefits can be innumerable, and lassoing the sunshine is all the easier.

**Sunset**

My hope is that the previous chapters have served to help you find a more positive approach to living. Relatively speaking, life is much too short to be hindered by unnecessary negativity. We all have a limited number of minutes on this planet, and as Coach Valvano said, we should strive to make the most of them. That is much more easily accomplished with a positive attitude and a strategy to glean the best from any given situation. One can expect a few clouds, rain showers, and even the occasional eclipse along the way, but fear not. We know the sun is still there, just waiting to peek out to provide the source of the magnificent rainbow.

The Man upstairs is pretty smart. If we try to ignore what the sunshine can do for us, if we try to look down to avoid the light, we see the darkness of our shadow. But that shadow is there because of the sun, and even that shadow can remind us of the power of the sun's teachings. May your shadow stand tall at sunrise, welcoming the new day and its challenges, anticipating all that you will accomplish. And may your shadow stand tall at sunset, proud of what you have done today, knowing tomorrow you can do more. May your shadow accompany you through your daily journey, sometimes behind you over your shoulder, sometimes in front leading the way, but always there and always reminding you that no shadow exists without the sun. Indeed, your shadow should be a constant reminder, not of the darkened silhouette that walks alongside you, but of the source that through its very light creates that darkness – the sun. Let your shadow be there to remind you of your daily approach to living – your approach to lasso the sunshine and capture the brighter side of life!

# Name Index

# Appendix

Many of the individuals discussed in this book have inspired me. I hope they have inspired you as well. Please find listed below some of the organizations that could use your help. Alternatively, if you have a favorite group or organization close to heart, please share the fruits of your labors with them. Donations may be made to the following addresses:

Southern Illinois Univ. School of Medicine
Foundation-Cancer Institute
927 N. Rutledge St.
Post Office Box 19666
Springfield, IL 62794-9666
Phone: 1-877-435-7766

The "V" Foundation for Cancer Research
100 Towerview Court
Cary, North Carolina 27513
Phone: 919-380-9505 (1-800-4JimmyV)
Fax: 919-380-0025
www.jimmyv.org

Hunter's Hope Foundation
Post Office Box 643
Orchard Park, New York 14127
Phone: 716-667-1200 (1-877-984-HOPE)
Fax: 716-667-1212
info@huntershope.org

Christopher Reeve Paralysis Foundation
636 Morris Turnpike, Suite #3A
Short Hills Plaza
Short Hills, New Jersey  07078
Phone:  1-800-539-7309
www.paralysis.org

American Diabetes Association
Attention: ADA Web
Post Office Box 1833
Merrifield, Virginia  22116
Phone:  1-800-DIABETES
1-800-342-2383
www.diabetes.org

The Susan G. Komen Breast Cancer Foundation
5005 LBJ Freeway, Suite 250
Dallas, TX 75244
Phone:  972-855-1600
www.komen.org